PROPHETIC:
HOW TO SPEAK WORDS THAT CHANGE LIVES

© BRIGHTHE@RT RESOURCES 2016

All quotations from the Bible are taken from *The Holy Bible: New International Version* ®. NIV®. Copyright © 2011, by International Bible Society.

TABLE OF CONTENTS:

INTRO: HIGH FIVE

PART ONE: FOUNDATIONS

Prophetic Purpose	6
Prophetic Sources	11
Prophetic Filters	15

PART TWO: WHERE TO START

Pray for life	22
Listen for life	26
How God speaks	30

PART THREE: GIVING & RECEIVING

Types of prophetic messages	36
Framing the message	39
Letting go	43
Receiving prophetic messages	45

PART FOUR: THE JOURNEY

Growing in the prophetic	50
Specialties and Gifting	54

High Five!

For many Christians, prophecy is kind of mysterious, a whole lot 'o' weird, and maybe even a little bit scary. If that describes you, you're not alone. But please… let me de-mystify prophecy for you forever.

Question: Have you ever looked ahead to an important conversation you needed to have with a friend and prayed, "God, please give me the right words to say?" or "Please speak through me?" or "God, I don't just want my words to just be my own?"

You have?

Well, that was a good prayer. Whether you realized it at the time, you were asking God to make your words *prophetic*.

And after that important conversation, did you marvel at the words that came out of your mouth, to the point that you even wondered, "Wow, I don't know where that came from! The words just kind of flowed!"

You have?

Well, congratulations again! That's because God answered your prayer—your words were prophetic, laced with wisdom from God.

And after those conversations, have your friends ever remarked, "Thank you. That was exactly what I needed to hear?"

What?! You've experienced that too? Well, time for a high five—not only were your words prophetic; your friend noticed, too.

So God used you, and it wasn't terribly mysterious, weird, or scary. It felt kind of… good. And you probably found yourself wishing you could experience more of whatever that was. Right?

While you congratulate yourself for your personal breakthrough, we need to move on—so here are a few words you'll need to understand from now on:

1. A *prophet* is someone who talks to people on God's behalf. All of us are supposed to do that but some of us have a special calling that takes it to the next level. More on this later.

2. Being *prophetic* means passing along what God tells us to say, how he tells us to say it.

3. A *prophecy* (or prophetic word) is the message we pass along.

4. When people talk about *"the"* prophetic they're talking about one or more of the first three things on this list.

So there you go. You're in the know.

Not so scary, right? Nope, not so scary at all. And the good news is, I'm pretty sure you've already done this. Probably more than once.

Now that we have that out of the way, how would you like to become *more* prophetic? Wouldn't it be amazing if God would speak through you on a regular basis? Wouldn't it be awesome to watch God speak life into death through the words that come out of your mouth?

Yeah, I'm totally with you on that. It would be fantastic.

Now, because there are so many different ideas about prophecy—some of which are twisted and can even be outright dangerous to our faith—it's important to lay a biblical foundation for the prophetic ministry. That way you can explore the prophetic knowing you're headed in the right direction. The Bible is a prophetic book that teaches us to live a prophetic life, after all. But I'm getting ahead of myself.

Ready? Let's dive in!

PART ONE: FOUNDATIONS

PROPHETIC PURPOSE

When you read a story, first impressions are everything.

The first time you meet a character in a book, the picture the author paints in your mind becomes the foundation for any new information you collect about them from then on. So on page one you realize the protagonist is a woman. In chapter two you learn she's a lawyer. In chapter three you see her character flaws beginning to emerge. By the time you turn the last page, you feel like you've known her all your life and hope the author is working on a sequel because she better not marry Jeb because he's dishonest and the new client might actually be right for her.

God lays out truths in the Bible the very same way. In the book of Genesis, starting from the opening line on page one, he patiently builds the picture of the world we live in, what went wrong, and how he is pursuing us to fix what we've broken. As we move through the Bible, the picture grows, comes to life, and becomes far more specific and detailed.

What does this have to do with prophecy? In Genesis chapter twenty, the very first mention of the prophetic sets the foundation of prophetic ministry for the rest of the Bible.

Abraham, one of God's first human friends, had moved to a foreign country with his wife, Sarai. She was drop-dead gorgeous, and Abraham thought there was a very real possibility that the locals would kill him to take her as their own. His solution? Pretend to be brother and sister. Abe convinced her to play along. What could possibly go wrong? The local King, Abimelech, rightly concluding the two were only siblings, snagged the new girl in town for his harem. Abraham got away scot-free, sure, but Sarai? Not so much.

> "But God came to Abimelech one night in a dream one night and said to him, "You are as good as dead because of the woman you have taken; she is a married woman." Now Abimelech had not gone near her, so he said, "Lord, will you destroy an innocent nation? Did he not say to me, 'She is my sister,' and didn't she also say, 'He is my brother'? I have done this with a clear conscience and clean hands." Then God said to him in the dream, "Yes, I know you did this with a clear conscience, and so I have kept you from sinning against me. That is why I did not let you touch her. Now return the man's wife, for **he is a prophet, and he will pray for you and you will live.** But if you do not return her, you may be sure that you and all who belong to you will die." (Genesis 20:3-7)

In spite of how painfully stupid Abraham's plan was, that it put his wife in mortal danger, and that it must have felt like an unforgivable betrayal to Sarai, this story lays the foundational framework for prophecy throughout the rest of the Bible.

Notice: Abimelech was in deep trouble, but God didn't want to judge him for it. He wanted to save him. And Abraham's prophetic role was to pray and say that stuff into the situation. *To speak life into death.*

We can't miss this! People all around us are stuck in sin, suffering from abuse, struggling with poor choices, and deserving of judgement—but God doesn't want to judge them. *He wants to save them.* He wants his light to pierce their darkness. He wants his joy to conquer their gloom, for his truth to replace their lies. He wants to set the captives free. Prophets speak life into death and invite people to respond to the loving God who's giving it.

Abraham's story is the first reference to prophecy in the entire Bible, and as such it sets the purpose of prophecy for us too. Even though most of us associate prophecy with judgement and the end of the world, God's original purpose for prophecy was to set people free to truly live. To thrive in life.

God builds on this foundation later on in the Old Testament, in Numbers 12:6. There he says, "**When there is a prophet**

among you, I, the Lord reveal myself to them in visions, I speak to them in dreams."

People need to hear from God, so he strategically places prophets *among* them. And then, with his prophets in place, he speaks light into darkness, life into death, hope into despair. Specifically, this verse says *God reveals himself to them and speaks to them.* So a prophet doesn't just relay messages. He or she gives others a better look at who God is and what he's saying.

Thousands of years later, Jesus, God's Son, was born. He was and still is the ultimate Prophet. Christ perfectly embodied the things we've learned so far:

- He came to give us *life.*
- He set aside his heavenly throne to live *among* us.
- While he walked this darkened earth he *revealed* the Father and spoke his words.

Jesus was the fulfillment of many ancient prophecies made throughout the generations that lived before him. But more importantly, *Jesus was the heart of prophecy, in the flesh.* This is why the apostle John wrote, "the spirit of prophecy is the testimony of Jesus" *(Revelation 19:10).*

The gospel (good news) of Jesus Christ is, at it's core, a prophetic message built on the same prophetic foundation we've been studying. It addresses our past, our present, and even our future! We're all like sheep who have gone astray, rebelling against God and deserving of judgement. But God doesn't want to judge us, he wants to save us. He loved the world so much that he sent his one and only Son, not just to pray for us so we could live like Abraham did for Abimelech, but to die for us so we could live... forever.

And that was just the beginning. God hasn't stopped loving the world. God loves the world so much that he's put *you* among people who are in trouble, people who are struggling, people who need you to speak good news into their bad news. People who need a better look at Jesus. And he calls you to be prophetic wherever you are. So the heart of prophecy is love! It's our motivation, our inspiration, and our goal. Period.

The Apostle Paul, building on the Old Testament foundation, made the purpose of prophecy even more specific: "The one who prophesies speaks to people for their strengthening, encouragement, and comfort" (II Cor. 14:3). There it is again: A prophet speaks strength into weakness, encouragement into discouragement, comfort into pain and grief. Do you want to love, strengthen, encourage, and comfort people? There are opportunities to be prophetic all around you!

A prophet in the Old Testament named Ezekiel experienced a powerful vision, where God invited him to prophesy life into death. This is what happened:

> "The hand of the Lord was on me, and he brought me out by the Spirit of the Lord and set me in the middle of a valley; it was full of bones. He led me back and forth among them, and I saw a great many bones on the floor of the valley, bones that were very dry. He asked me, "Son of man, can these bones live?"
>
> I said, "Sovereign Lord, you alone know."
>
> Then he said to me, "Prophesy to these bones and say to them, 'Dry bones, hear the word of the Lord! This is what the Sovereign Lord says to these bones: I will make breath enter you, and you will come to life. I will attach tendons to you and make flesh come upon you and cover you with skin; I will put breath in you, and you will come to life. Then you will know that I am the Lord.'"
>
> So I prophesied as I was commanded. And as I was prophesying, there was a noise, a rattling sound, and the bones came together, bone to bone. I looked, and tendons and flesh appeared on them and skin covered them, but there was no breath in them.
>
> Then he said to me, "Prophesy to the breath; prophesy, son of man, and say to it, 'This is what the Sovereign Lord says: Come, breath, from the four winds and breathe into these slain, that they may live.'" So I prophesied as he commanded me, and breath entered them; they came to life and stood up on their feet—a vast army" (Ezekiel 37:1-10).

Did you catch that? Prophetic words aren't just words. They carry the power of new life within them. As Jesus reminded his disciples, "the words I have spoken to you—they are full of the Spirit and life" (John 6:63). Ezekiel's experience teaches us that when we say what God wants us to say, things can happen that wouldn't have happened if we had stayed silent. Prophetic words are supernatural catalysts that can ignite a flame in the darkest valleys. This is a game-changer. Think of how many "Christians" seem to think its their job to judge sin, shame the sinner, condemn categories of sins, distance themselves from darkness, and make it abundantly clear they're better than unbelievers and would never do such sinful things. Think of how many "Christians" seem to relish the idea that God will judge their enemies, longing for the day when they'll finally be vindicated for all the wrongs done to them! Blech. That's not the gospel.

This doesn't mean prophecy never addresses sin or hard things. It means a prophet (from a human perspective) is someone who speaks God's good things into the hard things so people can choose fuller, richer lives in Christ.

Me? I want my words to strengthen, encourage, and comfort people. I want to speak life into death! In other words, I want to be more *prophetic*.

*

TRY THIS!

This week, something will frustrate you. People will behave badly and you may be offended or hurt. Instead of bringing a judgment focus to the situation, ask God, "What life do you want me to speak into this person/situation to strengthen, encourage, or comfort?" If God brings something specific to your mind to say to someone in particular, do it.

PROPHETIC SOURCES

Before you get too excited, I need to clarify something: *wanting* to be prophetic doesn't *make* you prophetic. Trying to be prophetic doesn't even make you prophetic. It just makes you creepy, pushy, or worse.

Not all 'prophecy' is from God. Sometimes people prophesy ideas homegrown from their own inspiration. God says of those people,

> "I have not sent them or appointed them or spoken to them. They are prophesying to you false visions, divinations, idolatries and the delusions of their own minds... yet they have run with their message; I did not speak to them, yet they have prophesied" (Jeremiah 14:14, 20:21).

Which is not exactly what we're aiming at. It's also possible for prophecy to be inspired by evil, deceiving spirits. John, one of Jesus' twelve disciples, wrote,

> "Dear friends, do not believe every spirit, but test the spirits to see whether they are from God, because many false prophets have gone out into the world" (I John 4:1).

This is clearly worse than making stuff up. It's being inspired by evil, which won't strengthen, encourage, and comfort people no matter how great the words sound. It will "steal, kill, and destroy" them over time because that's what the devil does (John 10:10). I'll teach you how to discern which source is inspiring a prophet or prophecy in the next chapter. For now, just note there are three sources for the prophetic: our own minds, deceiving spirits, and God.

So what makes a person authentically prophetic? Well, not a *what*, a *who*. Check out these verses:

"When the (Holy) Spirit rested on them, they prophesied" (Numbers 11:25).

"The Spirit of the Lord will come powerfully upon you, and you will prophesy with them; and you will be changed into a different person" (I Samuel 10:6).

"The Spirit also rested on them, and they prophesied in the camp" (Numbers 11:26).

"The Spirit of God came on Saul's men, and they also prophesied" (I Samuel 19:20).

"The Spirit of God came even on him, and he walked along prophesying" (I Samuel 19:23).

The pattern is powerful and clear: When the Holy Spirit comes upon us or rests on us, we become prophetic. In fact, that's one of the major reasons God gives us his Spirit.

I can hear you protesting, "Well, that's great, but I don't think the Holy Spirit has come upon me like that. So then this isn't really my thing." But hold on; God had Joel, one of his prophets in the Old Testament, prophesy an amazing promise:

"I will pour out my Spirit on all people. Your sons and daughters will prophesy, your old men will dream dreams, your young men will see visions. Even on my servants, both men and women, I will pour out my Spirit in those days" (Joel 2:28,29).

Did you catch that? God promised to pour out his Spirit on everyone—sons, daughters, young, old, men, women. You and me! Nobody gets left out. And the result, once again? *Everybody* who receives the Holy Spirit is going to prophesy.

Generations later, Jesus, the Ultimate Prophet, arrived on earth. He lived, he died, and rose again, commanding his disciples to wait for the Holy Spirit to come upon them. And then one day, KABOOM. The Holy Spirit filled all of them, and guess what? They spoke in tongues (a special form of prophecy). When the crowd that had gathered started asking, "What the...?!" Peter got up and connected the dots for them:

"This is what was spoken by the prophet Joel: "'In the last days, God says, I will pour out my Spirit on all people. Your sons and daughters will prophesy, your young men will see visions, your old men will dream dreams. Even on my servants, both men and women, I will pour out my Spirit in those days, and they will prophesy" (Acts 2:16-18).

If you've put your faith in Jesus, his Spirit has come to live inside of you. You are now prophetic because that's the effect he has on people. The Holy Spirit is the one who enables the prophetic to flow. He connects you to truth beyond you, truth from the heart of God. He gives you prophetic words to speak:

"What no eye has seen, what no ear has heard, and what no human mind has conceived"—the things God has prepared for those who love him—these are the things God has revealed to us by his Spirit. The Spirit searches all things, even the deep things of God. For who knows a person's thoughts except their own spirit within them? In the same way no one knows the thoughts of God except the Spirit of God. What we have received is not the spirit of the world, but the Spirit who is from God, so that we may understand what God has freely given us. This is what we speak, not in words taught us by human wisdom but in words taught by the Spirit, explaining spiritual realities with Spirit-taught words" (I Corinthians 2:9-13)

Amazing, right?

This means being prophetic isn't a state of mind. It's not a super-power or even just a spiritual gift that God gives us. Being prophetic is what flows naturally out of a growing relationship with God's Holy Spirit in us. It's about knowing Jesus, knowing his heart, and sharing what he reveals to us with others.

Jesus, the Ultimate Prophet, dwells in your heart by his Spirit (Ephesians 3:16,17). So yes—if you are a believer in Jesus, you have both the capacity and the calling to be prophetic. You can speak to people for their strengthening, encouragement, and comfort. You can speak life into death. That's what the Holy Spirit wants to do through you.

And get this: the moment you step out in faith as one of God's sons and daughters to "speak to people for their strengthening, encouragement, and comfort"—prophesying— you become a walking fulfillment of Joel's prophecy! Go back and re-read it again. This is your moment. God doesn't lie.

What he's waiting for is for you to surrender to him, to say yes to that prophecy and commit to growing into your part of the equation.

The next few chapters will explore what that means.

*

TRY THIS!

"Which of you fathers, if your son asks for a fish, will give him a snake instead? Or if he asks for an egg, will give him a scorpion? If you then, though you are evil, know how to give good gifts to your children, how much more will your Father in heaven give the Holy Spirit to those who ask him!" (Luke 11:11-13).

When we ask God for more of his Spirit, He loves to say yes. So do it! Tell him you're surrendering to his will and his power. Ask him to fill you with His Spirit so you can overflow with his prophetic love for people around you. Thank him for filling you and for releasing the prophetic in your life.

PROPHETIC FILTERS

Remember how I said first impressions lay a foundation for everything we learn after that? Well, pretty close to the beginning of the Old Testament, God makes it clear that not every prophet is the real deal. Some prophets are false, and their messages are too.

Scripture aside, you have your own impressions of the prophetic based on your personal experience. Those impressions, both good and bad, are effecting how you feel about what I'm writing right now. Maybe you grew up enjoying a rich heritage of hearing God and speaking his word. Maybe you've been wounded or turned off by people abusing the prophetic and find it difficult to talk about prophecy without an emotional reaction that predisposes you to seeing it through a suspicious filter.

Maybe you only have experience with false or even dangerous counterfeits of prophecy like consulting mediums, tarot cards, palm reading, etc. The Bible is very clear that these things are evil. God described Israel's most wicked King, Manasseh, this way:

> "He built altars to all the starry hosts. He sacrificed his children in the fire in the Valley of Ben Hinnom, practiced divination and witchcraft, sought omens, and consulted mediums and spiritists. He did much evil in the eyes of the Lord, arousing his anger" (II Chronicles 33:5,6).

Regardless of your past experience, I want you to lay your current filter at the feet of Jesus. Whether you're struggling with fear of the prophetic, personal woundedness from it, or even questioning whether your past experience is valid, we're all in the same boat. We all need to come to God's Word, the Bible, and submit our understanding to that truth. His truth will set us free to experience the prophetic the way he designed us to.

And with Jesus, we'll be safe. Throughout this book I'm going to show you why. Even more importantly, I'm going to show you how—starting with this: a powerful filter through which every single prophetic word we give or receive should be judged by. Here it is:

"If a prophet, or one who foretells by dreams, appears among you and announces to you a sign or wonder, and if the sign or wonder spoken of takes place, and the prophet says, "Let us follow other gods" (gods you have not known) "and let us worship them," you must not listen to the words of that prophet or dreamer" (Deuteronomy 13:1-3).

Did you catch that? Most people assume the number one filter is whether the words the prophet speaks come true or not. That's part of it, but it's not the primary filter. Why? Because some false words come true! No, according to this scripture, our primary and foolproof filter is this: When a prophetic word is inspired by the Holy Spirit, *it leads us to follow and worship God, the God of the Bible, more fully.*

"Okay," you might wonder. "But how do I know if it's leading me to follow and worship God or leading me away from him?" Good question! Just a few chapters later, in Deuteronomy 18:19-22, God breaks down this primary filter into three brilliant sub-filters. He says a prophetic word is leading us away from God, if...

1. "... A prophet... presumes to speak in my name anything I have not commanded,"

2. "... Or a prophet... speaks in the name of other gods,"

3. Or "If what a prophet proclaims in the name of the Lord does not take place or come true."

If any of these "Ifs" come into play, God says, "that is a message the Lord has not spoken. That prophet has spoken presumptuously, so do not be alarmed" (Deuteronomy 18:22). Let's unpack these three filters.

1. Anything I have not commanded.

At first this seems too obvious: *If God didn't say it, it's not from him.* When those words were written, God hadn't said very much. But as God continued to speak over the centuries in the Bible, this filter has gained a lot of power. We now have a complete biblical record full of things God has said. If a prophet says something that contradicts *any of* the expansive truth already revealed in scripture, it isn't God speaking, period. God may contradict our *interpretation* of scripture because we don't have perfect understanding, but he will never contradict himself and what he's said.

2. In the name of other gods.

Biblically speaking, someone's name is much more than something you write on a laniard when you attend a conference with people you don't know. A person or deity's name speaks to who they are—their character, their attributes, their power.

Now that God has revealed himself most fully in his Son, Jesus, who is "the radiance of God's glory and the exact representation of his being," (Hebrews 1:3) it's Christ's name and good news we measure everything against. To summarize, this is what Jesus offers:

Jesus lived the perfect life we could never live so he could give us the credit for it. Our goodness or righteousness is based on what he did for us, not what we do for God. This means we are eternally approved by God, right with him and validated so completely that we never have to prove ourselves again.

Jesus loved us so much that he died in our place to pay for sins we could never pay for. In him we are perfectly loved, accepted, and forgiven, restored to relationship with his Father and adopted into his family. We are his sons and daughers, so we don't live to please others, pay for our sins, or work for acceptance anymore.

Jesus rose from the dead, defeating death, sin, and satan, then shared this victory with us. This makes us overcomers who don't have to worry or try to be in control because Christ is victorious in us.

Jesus sent his Spirit to live in us and through us forever, which means we have eternal purpose (joining him in his mission), supernatural power, and fulfilment because of his presence in us. We don't live our lives to pursue lesser things to fill us.

Lastly, Jesus went to prepare heaven for us, so we are eternally secure and destined for glory, freeing us from having to possess all good things here and now.

If someone says something that seems true, but they say it in a way that contradicts who Jesus is and what he died to give us —if they embody the opposite spirit—it's not the Holy Spirit moving them to say what they're saying. So when a message comes to us, we need to ask, "Does this look, sound, and feel like Jesus and his good news?"

3. If what a prophet proclaims does not come true.

The first filter was about judging the word against what God has already said. The second filter was about judging the word against who God is. This final filter is about judging the word against your actual life. It's more than just whether the prediction *comes* true; it's whether the word spoken to you *rings* true. If a prophet says, "Your daughter will be rich one day," and you don't have a daughter, that's not God speaking. If he says, "You've been going through a hard time right now," and you've been having the time of your life, you get the idea—thumbs down. If what a prophet says doesn't *ring true* for you, either toss it or shelve it to see if it rings true later on in life.

On the other hand, if someone shares a prophetic word that affirms the truth of scripture, lines up nicely with who Jesus is and how he might speak, and resonates with your heart and life, pay attention. It could very well be God.

Once again, here's the filter:

1. Does it resonate with what God has already said?
2. Does it resonate with the character and work of Jesus?
3. Does it resonate with the life of the person receiving it?

I love how God reassures us after laying out this crucial filter. If a word fails the test, he says, "that prophet has spoken presumptuously, so do not be alarmed" (Deuteronomy 18:22). No need to freak out—just don't accept what they're saying. Walk away and forget about it.

In the Old Testament, though, when a prophet was found to be false, they were supposed to be put to death. Back then, prophets had to get it right one hundred percent of the time because they were some of God's only spokespeople. In other words, the people judged the prophets using the words they spoke.

In the New Testament, we're all called to be prophetic, and prophets aren't expected to get it right all the time. When they speak out in a group, for example, people are supposed to weigh what's been said, using the filter we just unpacked (I Corinthians 14:29).

One of the respected prophets in the New Testament church was a guy named Agabus. We have record of Agabus giving two prophetic words in the book of Acts. The first one was about a famine in the near future, which he got totally right (Acts 11:28). The second was about the Apostle Paul getting arrested in Jerusalem, which he got partly right, but most the major details were off (Acts 21:10-33).

The point is, they didn't kill Agabus or shun him for being a false prophet. This is because in the New Testament, prophets weren't the sole voice for God and learned to prophesy over time. The people around them who discerned the words they gave helped them grow into who they were called to be.

The beauty of this filter is that it works—both for the prophet discerning whether they should share what's on their mind, and for the person receiving a prophetic word. This means every message should be vetted twice: Once on *the way out of our mouth*, and a second time *on the way into someone else's heart.*

Isn't God brilliant?

*

TRY THIS!

When we ask God for more of his Spirit, He loves to say yes. So do it! Tell him you're surrendering to his will and his power. Ask him to fill you with His Spirit so you can overflow with his prophetic love for people around you. Thank him for filling you and for releasing the prophetic in your life.

If you're struggling with fear or a resistance to the prophetic, tell him that. But I dare you to say, "Jesus, I'm laying down my past experiences, disappointments, and reservations about the prophetic. I want what you have for me, nothing more, nothing less. In Jesus' name, amen."

PART TWO:
WHERE TO START

PRAY FOR LIFE

You tend to get more of what you focus on.

If you focus on building your marriage, your marriage will probably improve. If you look for the number seven, you're going to start seeing it everywhere. And if you believe God is always speaking, that you're wired to be prophetic, and that he wants to speak through you, you're going to find opportunities to do that.

On the other hand, if you wait for God to zap you or for people to come up to you and say, "God told me you're supposed to tell me what to do with my life," you're probably going to be waiting a very long time to activate the prophetic in your experience.

In fact, that's a great way of looking at the prophetic: Because the Spirit makes you prophetic, it's in you to give. But it's dormant until you activate it by responding to God in faith and opening your mouth.

Where should you start? Well, remember the very first verse about prophets in the Bible? It said, "He is a prophet, and he will pray for you and you will live" (Genesis 20:7). That's your entry point: Believing and accepting you're prophetic.

God wants to use your words to speak life into death. You don't have to be smart, witty, popular, good looking, experienced, or good with words. The Holy Spirit brings the presence of Jesus, the Ultimate Prophet, to life in you. So start praying for people. Do you see someone sitting alone looking discouraged? Pray that they would live. That they would experience the love and light of Jesus. Did you meet a rude, abrasive person? Pray they would experience the transforming love of Christ.

This alone will revolutionize your faith and turn your heart inside out. Why? Because your heart, without conscious focus in the other direction, is actively focused on itself.

If you own a retro stereo system, it may actually have a few dials instead of buttons or touch-screens. Your life is like one of those dials, except with just two possible settings:

In any given moment your heart is either set to give something or to get something.

If your heart is set on give, you're postured to let heaven flow into and through you. But if your heart is set on get, you've reversed the flow; you're looking to someone or something other than God to fill you. You're trying to suck things into yourself instead of giving things away. You're longing for others to speak into your life instead of looking for opportunities to speak into them. Our selfishness stops the flow of heaven cold.

We need to turn the dial to *give*.

How do we set our hearts on *give*? Is it even possible?

Yes. But the only way you can set your heart on *give* is to believe Jesus has either *met your* needs, is *meeting* your needs, or *will* meet your needs in the future. This frees you from having to get or take what you need from me or anyone else. You don't need to *get* something from anyone because you already *have* what you need.

This is the only way to truly and fully love someone, which is why Paul wrote, "Follow the way of love and eagerly desire the gifts of the Spirit, especially prophecy… the one who prophesies speaks to *people* for *their* strengthening, encouragement, and comfort" (I Corinthians 14:1,3). You can't truly see another person until you shift from wanting something *from* them to wanting something *for* them.

Being truly prophetic requires focusing on others instead of on ourselves. One chapter earlier, Paul writes, "If I have the gift of prophecy and can fathom all mysteries, and if I have a faith that can move mountains, but do not have love, I am nothing" (I Corinthians 13:1-3). Without love we're not making a difference; we're just making noise.

People gifted in the prophetic have told me the best prayer to pray is, "Jesus, help me to see people through your eyes. How do you see them?" When people talk, we can pray, "What are they really saying? What does their heart need right now? How can I love them?" During conversations with people I often pray, "Holy Spirit, give me wisdom. What am I missing? Guide me into truth."

Remember what Paul said:

> "What no eye has seen, what no ear has heard, and what no human mind has conceived" — the things God has prepared for those who love him — these are the things God has revealed to us by his Spirit. The Spirit searches all things, even the deep things of God. For who knows a person's thoughts except their own spirit within them? In the same way no one knows the thoughts of God except the Spirit of God. What we have received is not the spirit of the world, but the Spirit who is from God, so that we may understand what God has freely given us. This is what we speak, not in words taught us by human wisdom but in words taught by the Spirit, explaining spiritual realities with Spirit-taught words" (I Corinthians 2:9-13)

*

TRY THIS!

When you start giving as a way of life, your own selfishness will rise up to defend itself like a big, threatening wall. When you're hurt by someone, you'll think of yourself. When you're out for groceries and feel tired, you'll think of yourself. When you're together with friends and you've had a tough week, you'll ache for them to speak into your life, not the other way around. When you feel God prompting you to say something bold, you'll give in to fear to keep yourself comfortable.

This wall is your old self, your flesh, your sinful nature—and it's not the real you. The only way to get past it is to learn to trust what Jesus has done for you. Try praying these words out loud every day this week:

"Jesus, thank you for giving me your righteousness. I am validated, approved, and affirmed based on your work, not mine. Thank you for loving me so much that you gave your life to pay for my sins. I am forgiven, accepted, healed, and loved forever. Thank you for sharing your resurrection with me. I'm a conquerer, victorious, seated with you in heaven. Thank you for sending your Spirit to live in me. I am filled, complete, whole, empowered, satisfied, and sent as light into the darkness. Thank-you for going to prepare a place for me. I am eternally secure, destined to enjoy you and reign with you forever. In Jesus' name, amen!"

LISTEN FOR LIFE

One of the most important prophetic principles I can teach you is this:

There is a huge difference between discernment and prophecy.

If you don't grasp this concept, you'll end up speaking more death into death instead of speaking God's life into death.

Think of it like this: When you're sick, you go to the doctor. They listen to you, tap your kneecap, make you say "ahh," shine a stupid light in your eye, do a blood test, and offer a diagnosis for your symptoms. But they don't stop there, do they? A good doctor will give you a prescription to deal with the diagnosis. You already knew something was wrong; what you want to know is how to fix it.

Well, in spiritual terms, discernment is like a diagnosis, whereas prophetic words are like a prescription. Here's how they work together.

Let's say you get together for coffee with a friend you haven't seen in awhile. After ordering, you sit down and start to catch up—but something feels off. A few minutes in, you still sense it. They're being friendly enough and they don't seem to be mad at you, but there's a palpable heaviness surrounding them. Deeper into the conversation, you realize it's not heaviness, it's guilt and shame—almost like a dark, wet blanket sapping their life away. You're sure of it.

Assuming for a minute that your reading of the situation is accurate, the clarity you're getting is what we call discernment. It's how God helps us understand what's going on with situations and people. Every believer is called to develop discernment, and some believers even receive a special empowering or gifting to discern good and evil spirits. Discernment is so important!

But discernment isn't prophecy, and without making that distinction you might wait for a pause in the conversation and say, "I sense that you're filled with guilt and shame for something awful you've done. You've given the enemy a place in your life and it's sucking the life right out of you."

That may be the truth, but Jesus isn't *only* the truth. He's also the *way* and the *life* (John 14:6). That means he doesn't just show us the gap between the difficult truth we're living and the elusive life we long for. He shows us the *way to bridge the gap.*

The "most excellent way," the way of prophecy, is love (I Corinthians 14:1). This is why Paul says we're supposed to speak the truth in love (Eph. 4:15). It's why Jesus came from the Father, "full of grace and truth" (John 1:14). Truth without grace can only condemn us. Truth wrapped in grace sets us free.

At the creation of the cosmos, the Spirit of God hovered over the darkness. But he didn't stop there. In a moment of glory, he spoke life into the blackness: "Let there be light" (Genesis 1:1-3).

Eons later, he hovered again over the darkness of our world and sent his Son into it to speak love and life into humanity. We became believers because "God, who said, "Let light shine out of darkness," made his light shine in our hearts to give us the light of the knowledge of God's glory displayed in the face of Christ" (II Corinthians 4:6).

And now, Jesus lives in you, and sends you into that same darkness to speak his love and light into other people's hearts. This doesn't minimize sin or erase the need for people to repent of their sin—it just makes God's love and goodness the most important ingredient in life change.

If this makes you uncomfortable, the Apostle Paul would ask, "Do you show contempt for the riches of his kindness, forbearance and patience, not realizing that God's kindness is intended to lead you to repentance?" (Romans 2:4). It's the good news in Christ that gives us both the perspective on and ability to repent of our bad news.

Does that make sense?

Let's you've discerned some darkness lingering over your coffee buddy. Maybe you even sense some sin, struggle, or a spiritual bondage involving the enemy. That's not the word you're supposed to share. Why? because it's *bad news*. Jesus is the gospel, the *good news*. So when you discern bad news, you need to ask the Holy Spirit to give you the good news God has to address that bad news. That's the message you're called to speak. We speak life into death. This is why Peter, describing the gospel of Jesus' death and resurrection, said,

"We also have the prophetic message as something completely reliable, and you will do well to pay attention to it, as to a light shining in a dark place, until the day dawns and the morning star rises in your hearts. Above all, you must understand that no prophecy of Scripture came about by the prophet's own interpretation of things. For prophecy never had its origin in the human will, but prophets, though human, spoke from God as they were carried along by the Holy Spirit" (II Peter 1:19-21).

The gospel is prophetic message for a couple of reasons.

First of all, it fulfills a boatload of prophecies throughout the Bible.

Secondly, Jesus, the Ultimate Prophet, is the embodiment of the good news.

Third, the gospel says, "You're living in bad news, but the good news can change your present, transform your past, and liberate your future!"

Fourth, when people respond to the gospel, they are fulfilling prophecy by finding their place in God's promises about them. Isn't that powerful?

But I'm really getting ahead of myself. Let's take some time to talk about what kinds of "prophetic words" God gives us for people.

*

TRY THIS!

Think of someone who rubs you the wrong way or has done something to irritate or offend you recently. Instead of nursing a grudge, repent of seeing them through your own eyes and easy God to show you how he sees them. Ask the Holy Spirit, "What is the light you would like to speak into this darkness?" When something comes to you, write it down. If it passes the prophetic filters test, step out and share it with the person in love and see what God does with it.

How God Speaks

Some of you are probably wondering, "How am I supposed to pass on a message from God if I don't hear his voice myself?"

Am I right?

Or, when I say God "speaks" or when I mention his "voice" you may not be totally clear about what I'm talking about. So let's make it as clear as possible. Some of you already hear from God, but there's always more to learn!

First of all, God *is* talking to you. Jesus said, "My sheep listen to my voice. I know them, and they follow me" (John 10:27). If you belong to Jesus, if you've put your faith in him, you're one of his sheep. Which means you hear his voice.

"But I *don't*," you might be thinking. "I mean sure, there have been moments, but they're rare, and God doesn't really talk to me."

Okay… I'm not sure how to say this without sounding rude, but you're wrong. And that's great news! Jesus said you hear him, and Jesus is right, because he *is* the truth (John 14:6). That's the first thing you need to accept: Your problem isn't hearing God's voice. It's *recognizing* his voice.

One of the fundamentals of communication is that you cannot not communicate. Even when your friend gives you the silent treatment, they're saying a whole lot, right? It's the same with God. Everything he does (or doesn't do) communicates something important. While people are often unaware of how and what their body language, tone of voice, and behaviour is communicating, God is perfectly, strategically aware of every message he's sending.

When we say God speaks, what we're really saying is that God communicates. He's communicating with you continuously, and his messages arrive packaged in five different forms. Let's unwrap them, one at a time.

WORDS

God speaks verbally. This one is the most obvious. The Bible is the best example of God's verbal communication, because "all scripture is inspired by God" (II Timothy 3:16,17) and perfectly communicates his truth in a way that transcends time, space, and culture. It's *universal*, so it becomes the standard by which everything else we think we hear God saying is evaluated.

But God's verbal communication is also *personal.* Jesus says, "He calls his own sheep by name and leads them out" (John 10:3). Some might say that God speaks every language, so that everyone everywhere can hear him. But it's better than that: God speaks *your* language, so that you can understand him. He knows your vocabulary, your experiences, and your mental filters—and uses them as the framework for his communication with you. God's personal communication unpacks and applies what he's already revealed in the Bible.

PICTURES

God also speaks visually—either through what we see around us, or by evoking pictures in our minds. For example, when God spoke to Jeremiah, he gave him a picture:

"The word of the Lord came to me: "What do you see, Jeremiah?"

"I see the branch of an almond tree," I replied.

The Lord said to me, "You have seen correctly…" (Jeremiah 1:11,12).

Whether Jeremiah is looking at an actual almond tree or whether God put one in his imagination, the message is still valid. I think lots of people get pictures from God but don't realize this is one of the beautiful ways he's speaking to them.

At other times, God speaks more directly into people's minds, giving us what we call dreams or visions. Visions are pictures or 'movies' that capture the person's mind so profoundly that they aren't just 'imagining' the images—it's more like being immersed in virtual reality while the vision is unfolding.

LOGIC

Another common way God's voice slips under our radar is through our logic. One of the most common misconceptions about the voice of God is framed in a typical question: "How do I know whether it's God speaking or just my own thoughts?"

Well, who says it can't be both?

Jesus says his Holy Spirit "will guide you into all truth" (John 16:13). Sometimes God 'drops' words or pictures into our minds, depositing the truth *into us.* This verse implies the opposite—that God also guides *us* into truth by guiding our thought process in the right direction. Because the guiding process is more subtle, we often don't realize God is speaking to us through our own ideas. Peter, one of Jesus' twelve disciples, experienced this kind of revelation. He had been with Jesus for several years, slowly coming to grips with who Jesus was. Then, one day, Jesus asked,

> "Who do you say I am?"
> Simon Peter answered, "You are the Messiah, the Son of the living God."
> Jesus replied, "Blessed are you, Simon son of Jonah, for this was not revealed to you by flesh and blood, but by my Father in heaven" (Matthew 16:15-17).

I love this story, because Jesus had to help Peter realize God had been speaking to him through his own thought process. His logic!

INTUITION

Another way God speaks to us is through our intuition. There are no words, no pictures, no real thought process: we just suddenly know something that we didn't know before. We don't know how we know, we just... do.

This happened to Jesus a lot. For example, there were moments where we read, "Jesus, knowing their thoughts..." (Luke 9:4). He didn't read their minds. He just knew. How? God revealed it to him.

Have you ever been about to do something, when out of the blue, you quoted Han Solo from Star Wars? "I have a bad feeling about this." That's what I'm talking about.

Intuitive messages from God can get mixed up with our own fears and filters. Sometimes we're just reading our own emotions and jump to conclusions God isn't wanting us to grab hold of. Intuitive messages from God need a lot more testing before we run with them, but they're still valid and real.

TOUCH

Actions really can speak louder than words. Reaching out and giving someone a compassionate hug often says more than words ever could! God may whisper "I love you" into your heart, but Jesus dying in your place on the cross is the ultimate demonstration of God's love for you (Romans 5:8-10).

God still speaks to us through physical touch. Sometimes we 'feel' his presence. Other times his guidance is accentuated by a physical sensation, like a knot in our stomach when we know something we want to do is wrong for us. Other times, joy washes over us. When God heals our bodies, that's not just a healing; it's also a message.

John, one of Jesus' first twelve disciples, had a vision of Jesus that totally messed him up: "When I saw him, I fell at his feet as though dead." But Jesus didn't stop there: "Then *he placed his right hand on me* and said: "Do not be afraid." (Revelation 1:17).

It was the *touch* of Jesus that gave John courage.

So there you have it—five ways God has already been speaking to you. But let me point out two more keys that will unlock this truth for you.

First, God often 'bundles' his communication in multiple packages. In the last example, John saw, heard, and felt Jesus communicating with him. Afterwards, the Holy Spirit guided John into more truth (logic) as he reflected on what he'd seen and heard. This will happen to you as well.

Second, while God uses all five modes of communication, you'll probably notice one or two of them seem to be more regular channels than others. I have a friend who really leans into the visual. I tend to hear words and pictures. Others tend to be logic people. You get the idea.

In the next section, we'll explore what to do with all this. It's vital that you learn to tune in to the ways God is already speaking to you. If you don't learn to recognize God's voice, the practical effect will be the same as if he isn't speaking at all!

*

TRY THIS!

Spend some time right now reflecting on ways God may have been trying to get your attention or send you a message of some kind. For example, do you think he might be trying to speak to you through this book? What is God saying? How is he packaging it?

- Is it coming directly through the *words* you're reading?
- Is it coming through a train of *thoughts* (logic) building on what you're reading?
- Have there been *pictures* or images in your mind as you read?
- Has God been helping you realize things about yourself and the way he works *(intuition)*?
- Have you experienced any *physical* sensations or emotions as you read (heat, goosebumps, joy, peace)?

Talk to him about any of these that you think might be God communicating with you!

PART THREE:
GIVING & RECEIVING

TYPES OF PROPHETIC MESSAGES

We've learned that God speaks in at least five different ways. Regardless of how the truth comes to you, when he speaks to you about someone else and moves you to pass on what you've heard, you'll have to translate the ideas into words. But don't worry, the Holy Spirit will guide and inspire you.

There are four basic types of prophetic messages the Holy Spirit gives us. Knowing what they are and what they're for will help you identify how God may want to use you.

WORDS OF KNOWLEDGE

"To one there is given through the Spirit… a message of knowledge…" (I Corinthians 12:8). Words of knowledge are bits of information God reveals to us about people or situations that we couldn't know otherwise. The purpose of a word of knowledge is to get people's attention and wake them up to the fact that God loves and knows them intimately.

If God gives me a word of knowledge about you—say, what happened in your first year of college—the real message isn't in the information I shared, it's in the fact that God revealed it. It shows he cares, that he sees, that he knows. This can be life-changing for people. Paul puts it this way:

"If an unbeliever or an inquirer comes in while everyone is prophesying, they are convicted of sin and are brought under judgment by all, as the secrets of their hearts are laid bare. So they will fall down and worship God, exclaiming, "God is really among you!" (I Corinthians 14:24,25).

A word of knowledge often paves the way for words of wisdom, prophecy, healing, or other miracles by opening people's hearts to divine possibilities and building their faith.

WORDS OF WISDOM

"To one there is given through the Spirit a message of wisdom" (I Corinthians 12:8). A word of wisdom is divinely inspired insight into someone's life, struggles, or decision-making. Think of words of wisdom as missing puzzle pieces, or clarity that helps people connect the dots in their world. It's how God turns the lights on for someone, giving them the "aha!" moment they've been looking for.

Typically a word of wisdom empowers or frees a person to move forward where they have been stuck, hurt, confused, or stagnant. In other words, words of wisdom are usually about the *past* or the *present.*

PROPHECY

In one sense, prophecy describes all forms of the prophetic. But in other places in scripture, it's used to describe a word of wisdom that pertains to the *future.* The night Jesus was arrested before his crucifixion, Jesus warned his disciples about what was going to happen.

"Peter declared, "Even if all fall away, I will not."
"Truly I tell you," Jesus answered, "today—yes, tonight—before the rooster crows twice you yourself will disown me three times." (Mark 14:29,30).

When this scenario played out later that night, Peter realized to his horror what he'd done and cried like a baby. How could knowing this strengthen, encourage, and comfort Peter?

Let me put it this way: While Peter's failure caused a whole lot of soul searching, Jesus was showing Peter, "I know you. I know you aren't perfect. In fact, you'll deny me three times! But I still love you. I'm still trusting my kingdom mission to you. It's not based on your performance. It's based on my grace." This was a message that made little sense for Peter at the time, but would resonate in a big way later on when times got really tough.

TONGUES

Sometimes God wraps his messages in a different language that requires somebody else to interpret (I Corinthians 14:27). This can be a heavenly language not found on earth that the hearer is empowered by God to understand (I Corinthians 13:1); other times, it's a human language the speaker didn't learn but the listener already knows (Acts 2:4-12).

While many people are able pray in tongues, not everyone has the gift of tongues. What's the difference? When someone prays in tongues, they are speaking *to God* (and) no one understands them; they utter mysteries with their spirit" (I Corinthians 14:2). When someone has the gift of tongues, they speak publicly *to people* on behalf of God, and someone interprets the message so others can understand it (I Corinthians 14:27, 28). In other words, praying in tongues is personal; the gift of tongues is public.

*

TRY THIS!

Think back to review any experiences you may have had with God speaking through you. This could include moments when you sensed wisdom that was not your own flowing through your words, or when people remarked, "That was just what I needed to hear." Spend a few minutes categorizing these experiences with the four types I've outlined here: words of knowledge, words of wisdom, prophecy, and tongues.

If you can't remember experiences like this, maybe you've experienced moments when others have spoken into your life with words from God. Try to categorize those moments. Thank God for the ways he speaks!

FRAMING THE MESSAGE

Let's not leave your friend (from a few chapters back) hanging out to dry.

You were out for coffee, remember? You sensed some real heaviness and darkness in their life (that's an intuitive message from God). So you started to pray for them. Good for you!

Maybe, as you pray, you get a picture in your mind of Jesus coming behind them and lifting the shameful blanket from their shoulders and whispering, "It's over. It's gone." That's a picture, combined with words. A word of wisdom.

Time to share it, right? Not yet. Let's run it through the three prophetic filters first:

1. Does it resonate with what God has already said? Yes.
2. Does it resonate with the character and work of Jesus? Yes.
3. Does it resonate with their actual life? It seems to.

If #3 checks out, the message would certainly strengthen, encourage, and comfort them, right? This is definitely worth sharing to see if it resonates, but how we frame the words we share is just as important as the word itself. We need speak the truth (that's the word), but we also need to make sure we speak it in love (that's the framing).

First of all, ask God what you should do with the word he's put on your heart. Don't assume you know; assume you don't! He may just want you to pray the word into someone's life.

Timing is also important. Just because God put something into your mind doesn't mean you need to share it right away.

Second, check your motives. Are you trying to correct the person? Put them in their place? Win an argument? Control their behaviour? None of those things are grounded in love. Love wants to see them strengthened, encouraged, or comforted. In other words, to see them built up and empowered. This is not a technicality; its the whole point!

But let's go back to your friend, the one sitting across from you sipping coffee. Let's assume God wants you to share the message with them during this coffee time. How do you "bring up" what you believe God is putting on your heart to say? You can certainly pray for an opening in a conversation, but either way you'll have to clear you throat and just go for it.

Ready with what seems like God's good news for their heaviness, now you might ask, "Hey, are you okay? It seems to me like there's a kind of heaviness about you."

You're testing your discernment here. Discernment, as we've seen, isn't the message; it's the starting point. Words of knowledge often fall into this category as well.

Do you notice how natural this can be? You took a bit of a risk, but you didn't put on a "prophet voice" or begin with "Thus says the Lord...". You didn't even say, "God is telling me." Why? Because you only *think* God is telling you. You're testing out a word of knowledge here, and you might have gotten it wrong.

When you claim to be God's mouthpiece, what you're implying is that the person has to listen to what you have to say and follow you—which is the opposite of what God is trying to impart. He's trying to set them free to take personal responsibility for their relationship with him.

They sigh and confess, "Yeah, that's exactly how I feel." So your discernment is accurate, which means the message you want to share might just be accurate too.

"I'm not sure what that's all about," you say, "but as we were talking I got this picture in my mind of Jesus coming behind you and lifting something like a heavy blanket off of your shoulders and whispering, "It's over. It's gone." Does that make any sense to you?"

Please notice: You shared the message, not the interpretation, because that's all God revealed to you. God told Jeremiah to give prophets these instructions: "Let the prophet who has a dream recount the dream, but let the one who has my word speak it faithfully" (Jeremiah 23:28). In other words, the dream (or message) is one thing; the interpretation is another.

So back to your friend: You've shared the picture and the words you believe God laid on your heart. And you've just asked, "Does that make any sense to you?"

"Wow, yeah, it does." He tears up. "I really needed to hear that."

"How so?"

"A few months ago I really screwed up in my marriage and my wife forgave me and everything, but I just can't forgive myself. The guilt is suffocating. It's been a rough road."

What a confirmation of the message! Sensing God's love for them, you reach across the table and put your hand on their shoulder. "I'm so sorry." Which is also a kind of physical message from God to them.

Even in this little made-up scenario, there is a lot of prophetic messaging going on—and yet it's so natural and simple when the Holy Spirit is using us to strengthen, encourage and comfort someone.

I often hear people prophesy without realizing it, in particular while they're praying for someone out loud. When people shift from asking God for things ("Please give Bob strength, Lord!") to stating things ("Please show Bob that you're right there, reaching out to him") it means they're seeing that picture in their minds and are incorporating it into their prayer.

When that happens to you, here's a rule of thumb to clarify what to do with it: If you have something to pray, pray it; if you have something to say, say it. I often "get" something from God while I'm praying for someone. When that happens I try to pause the prayer and say, "Bob, I just sense that God is right here with you, reaching out to you." Then I keep praying.

It's important to separate prayer and the prophetic, because even though they ripple back and forth into each other, when we pause like that and give God's messages their own platform, people are more likely to receive it as a message from God.

While I was writing this little chapter, I stepped out of my office to join a conversation where my wife, Shauna, spoke some powerful prophetic words into my adult son's life. I had started to speak what I felt were important ideas, but they weren't connecting. Then she stepped up, and BOOM. The love was flowing, God's presence was obvious, and the result was amazing. I praise God for her!

Afterwards I reflected on why my words fell flat while hers empowered my son to rise to a new challenge. "She was trying to love him, and you were trying to correct and change him," the Holy Spirit chided me. Yup. That's about right! That's why love is so important in framing what we say.

Isn't God good?

*

TRY THIS!

1. When you sense a message from God for someone, test it with the three filters.

2. If it passes the test, ask the Holy Spirit what to do with it.

3. Pray for the right timing and a heart overflowing with love for the person.

4. If you're supposed to share it to strengthen, encourage, or comfort them, only share what God revealed to you—not what you think it means or what you think they should do about it.

5. Talk in your own, relaxed voice, motivated by love for the person you're sharing it with.

6. If you have something to pray, pray it. If you have something to say, say it.

LETTING GO

So... you've listened and prayed for God's good news for someone, tested it, and shared it with them.

Now what?

Now... you let it go. You've done your job; now it's time for the other person to do theirs.

But... What if they don't pay attention to what you've said? What if they forget to pray about it? What if they don't do anything with it and miss out on what God wants for them?

What happens next is entirely up to them. But this is a good thing. Imagine you're the one receiving a prophetic message. Would you want the person to follow up, hound you, nag you, guilt you, and push you to take their advice? No, you wouldn't.

After Shauna spoke into my son's life, she let go. She let him process it and respond to the message in his own way. And you know what? He went out immediately, took action on the message, and took a major step forward in his life! If we had told him what to do, forced him into action, and nagged him until he did it, the win wouldn't have been his. It would have been ours, and he wouldn't have grown further into the man God knows he can be.

Love doesn't control people. It doesn't even try.

The exhilarating, frustrating, beautiful truth is that people get to choose. It's not your job to make sure people listen. It's your job to speak the truth in love. And then, it's your job to...

Let.

It.

Go.

Do you know why? Because you're not the Holy Spirit, and you can't do his job. When we try to do his job, we get in his way, and often make it harder for the person to see the truth.

*

TRY THIS!

Think about someone you've tried to share a "God message" with, or maybe just "talk some sense into," but they didn't receive it well or do anything about it.

How did that feel? How *does* that feel? When this happens, you'll be tempted to ascribe your own emotional response to God. "God is so angry right now that you didn't listen! You're going to miss out!"

The truth is, any frustration, anger, rejection, or hurt you experienced as a result of their less than amazing response is *your* issue, not theirs. You just bumped into your own insecurities and control issues.

So... You need to confess your sinful attitude, including your lack of faith in the Holy Spirit. You need to confess that your heart has shifted from loving the person to controlling them. You need to step off the throne and let Jesus sit there so you can bow before him in worship and trust.

So do that. Here is a prayer that models how this could work:

Lord Jesus, I'm sorry that I let my insecurities overwhelm my love for this person. I really wanted them to listen and accept the message I gave them, but I shifted from loving them to controlling them. I am not the Holy Spirit, so I'm getting out of the way. It's up to you to guide them into the truth, not me. Jesus, I choose to stand down, trust you, and love them no matter what. In your name, Jesus, Amen.

RECEIVING PROPHETIC MESSAGES

So far you've been learning how to share prophetic messages with others. Now it's time to look in the mirror.

What if *you're* the person who's been asked out for coffee? What if your friend shifts the conversation and asks, "Hey, are you okay? It seems to me like there's a kind of heaviness about you."

What then?

You're in the driver's seat. You can choose whether to respond to the question, how deep to go with your reply, and whether you want to change the subject.

You don't know they're being prophetic at this point. All you know is that they care about how you're doing. But if I were you, if they're reading you right, I'd be honest about it.

"Yeah, that's exactly how I feel."

"I'm not sure what that's all about," they reply, "but as we were talking I got this picture in my mind of Jesus coming behind you and lifting something like a heavy blanket off of your shoulders and whispering, "It's over. It's gone." Does that make any sense to you?"

As they relay the message, it's up to you to listen. If they truly understand the prophetic, they will share the message and let it sit, not adding their two cents about what it should mean to you or what you should do about it.

This the point where you need to test the word for yourself. If they understand healthy prophetic 'protocol,' they will have tested the message internally *before speaking it*, but you still need to test it yourself *before receiving it*. Remember the three-fold filter test?

1. Does it resonate with what God has already said?
2. Does it resonate with the character and work of Jesus?
3. Does it resonate with my actual life?

At this point, there are three possible options. One, the word fails one or more questions on the test, meaning you should reject it. If that's the case, you can politely say, "Wow, that's really interesting. I don't think that's what God is saying to me, but thank you for sharing that with me." You're not just *allowed* to give honest feedback; you *need* to give honest feedback so they can grow in their ability to hear God and share what's on his heart.

A second option would be that it passes the first two questions, but it doesn't resonate with your actual life. At this point you can say, "Wow, that's really interesting. It could definitely be from God, although it doesn't really line up with my life right now (or part of it does, but part of it doesn't). I'm going to pray about it and see if it comes back around in the future. Thank you for sharing that with me."

In the case we've been pretending through, the message got three green lights: It resonates with the Bible, who Jesus is, and your actual life. The message is probably from God—but you can still choose what to do with it. It's not up to them to discern that.

Let's say you choose to trust this person, seeing as they appear to be speaking truth from God.

"Wow, yeah, it does resonate." You feel yourself tear up. "I really needed to hear that."

"How so?" they ask.

Again, you get to choose. You can say, "I'd rather not talk about it," or you can open up further. Personally, when God is speaking into my life through another person, I try to fling open the doors of my heart as wide as possible because I want every single ounce of what God has for me.

But it's up to you.

"A few months ago I really screwed up in my marriage," you say. "My spouse forgave me and everything, but I just can't forgive myself. The guilt is suffocating. It's been a rough road."

Your friend reaches across the table and puts their hand on your shoulder. "I'm so sorry," they say. And remember how God speaks: words, pictures, intuition, logic, and touch. Even that 'shoulder squeeze' is a message from God through that person. He loves you!

After the coffee, it's up to you to pray about it. To follow through. To get some counselling for unresolved guilt. You get the picture. You get to choose, but if God is really speaking, you need to listen and obey. Your future depends on it. As Jesus said,

"All who listen to my instructions and follow them are wise, like a man who builds his house on solid rock. Though the rain comes in torrents, and the floods rise and the storm winds beat against his house, it won't collapse, for it is built on rock. "But those who hear my instructions and ignore them are foolish, like a man who builds his house on sand. For when the rains and floods come, and storm winds beat against his house, it will fall with a mighty crash" (Matthew 7:24-27).

There are all kinds of reasons people ignore what God is saying. Sometimes we don't like what we're hearing. Other times we don't want to give up something he's asking for, or we're afraid to do something he's calling us to do. That said, it's vitally important that we listen carefully to God, hanging on his every word, obeying what he says:

"Today, if you hear his voice, do not harden your hearts...your ancestors tested and tried me... I said, 'Their hearts are always going astray, and they have not known my ways.' ...So I declared on oath in my anger, 'They shall never enter my rest.' " (Hebrews 4:7-9,11).

Aristotle described the word 'anger' used here as "desire with grief." God aches for us to listen to his voice! And this really is between you and God. You never have to be psyched out or intimidated by the prophetic—even if some high-powered, self-proclaimed prophet with bad breath gets in your face and bellows, "Thus saith the Lord!!!" and expects you to listen up... and listen good!!

No matter what, you get to choose. You get to discern. You get to respond the way you sense God leading you to respond. You answer to Jesus, not the person giving the word.

Jesus began his prophetic ministry by calling people to "repent and believe" (Mark 1:15). The response God wants from you is repentance, regardless of whether the message you received was challenging (calling out your sin) or encouraging (lifting your spirits). This is because the truth God is sending is replacing a lie that's been producing bad fruit in your life. The message is meant to change your heart mind, and direction.

For example, your buddy shared a message from God with you, a picture "of Jesus coming behind you and lifting something like a heavy blanket off of your shoulders and whispering, "It's over. It's gone." You've been living with guilt, not believing in Christ's forgiveness. You'll need to repent of believing the lie that Jesus isn't enough to truly embrace the freeing truth: "It's gone."

The key is to be open to what God may be saying at all times, living to receive every word that comes from the mouth of God (Matthew 4:4) and testing every message that comes your way.

*

TRY THIS!

Ask the Holy Spirit, "Lord, have you been trying to talk to me through people around me? If there's a message I've missed, could you please remind me of that?" When someone shares what might be a message with you, test it with the three filters:

1. Does it resonate with what God has already said?
2. Does it resonate with the character and work of Jesus?
3. Does it resonate with my actual life?

If it passes the filter test, God is talking to you, which means you're not done yet. Now it's time to talk to God about what to do with what he's saying. Start by asking him that simple question: "God, thank you for speaking to me. Please guide me now. What would you like me to do with this?"

Repent of what you've been believing, and welcome the truth into that empty space. Then follow Jesus where he leads.

PART FOUR: THE JOURNEY

GROWING IN THE PROPHETIC

If you haven't picked up on the obvious yet, let me spell it out: I want you to embrace the prophetic as a normal part of what it means to follow Jesus.

I'm praying that this book will ignite a spark within you, that you'll grab hold of Jesus' invitation to "follow the way of love and eagerly desire gifts of the Spirit, especially prophecy," (I Corinthians 14:1). Why? Because God wants you to prophesy. He wants you to speak words that build people up—strengthening, encouraging, and comforting them. And the world needs you to prophesy—to speak words of life into death, light into darkness.

The good news is, God doesn't expect you to get it right all the time or to bat one hundred percent. He knows growing in your ability to be prophetic is a lifelong journey, and he's committed to walk that path with you. Every single step. Here are two important principles that will keep you growing without getting derailed along the way.

AMONG

In Numbers 12:6, God says, "When there is a prophet *among* you, I, the Lord, reveal myself to them in visions, I speak to them in dreams." This verse establishes an important principle: When God wants to speak light into darkness in people's lives, he puts a prophet among them. That's what you are: God's messenger, strategically placed among people who need his truth spoken in love. I've written this book to help you accept that epic calling.

The flip side of this truth is that when prophets are listening to God, they are firmly planted among people. They are living in community as integral members of families, groups, cultures, and neighbourhoods. Just like Jesus, the Ultimate Prophet, humbled himself and became one of us and lived among us (John 1:14), we need to humble ourselves and remember we are one of the people we live with—no better than anyone else. We need people just as much as they need us.

Prophetic people live in community and submit to the community. They don't separate or elevate themselves from the people they are called to love.

This means you need to be *socially* connected as a fully-committed 'member' of a local church, submitted to it's leadership. It also means you need to be *personally* connected, known by a smaller group of people within that church. Within that smaller group, you need to be *intimately* connected with two or three people who love you enough to hold you accountable.

If you aren't connected on these three levels, that's mission number one. Jesus said that listening to his voice as a flock of sheep is safe, but he did mention false shepherds, thieves, strangers, and wolves who try lead us astray to eat us for breakfast (John 10:1-12). The strategy of the wolf? he "attacks the flock and *scatters* it."

This is critical, so please hear me: When you're tempted to withdraw from social, personal, and intimate relationships within the church, *you are under attack.* Every step you take away from healthy community is listening to the enemy's voice. You are being scattered and lured into isolation where he can deceive you and take you out of the battle.

Remember, God puts prophets *among* people.

CORRECTION

No one like to be wrong, and we hate being corrected for being wrong even more. The problem is, correction is a crucial part of growth. The Apostle Paul says,

"You have known the Holy Scriptures, which are able to make you wise for salvation through faith in Christ

Jesus. All Scripture is God-breathed and is useful for teaching, rebuking, correcting and training in righteousness, so that the servant of God may be thoroughly equipped for every good work" (II Timothy 3:15-17).

The only way to be thoroughly equipped for every good work, which would include prophetic ministry, is to be taught, rebuked, corrected, and trained. Sounds like fun, right?

I once knew a pastor who's church leadership team never used phrases like "I think God wants" or "I was praying and God laid this on my heart." His reasoning was that as soon as you invoke the "God said" clause, the conversation is over. How can you dare question what God has spoken?

I see his point, but the New Testament approach is to encourage people to speak what they think is from God and then weigh what is said, like we've been talking about. Paul gave this advice to people who were just learning to use their spiritual gifts, including prophetic ones: "Love must be sincere. Hate what is evil; cling to what is good" (Romans 12:4-9). A prophetic word isn't a conversation *ender;* it's a conversation *starter.*

One of the reasons we need to be actively engaged in healthy relationships is that we also need honest feedback about the messages we're learning to share. If we mean well but are off base, we need to be corrected. If we're way out of line, a loving rebuke is in order.

The best way to receive helpful feedback is to ask for it. When you deliver a message, ask, "Does that resonate with you?" If it doesn't, don't try and force the message on the person. Say, "Hmmm, okay. I'm learning to hear God's voice and I thought this might be a word from him. Thanks for letting me practice."

Another important way to receive correction is to track the words you give people. Write down the details and come back around to them at a later date. "Hey, last year I shared that word with you. Did anything ever happen with that?" And be humble if there is something to apologize for. Learn from the experience. If your words never "land"—never resonate, you may want to go back the the drawing board and learn to discern God's voice more accurately.

Another important aspect to growing in the prophetic is learning how and when it is appropriate to bring messages from

God. Paul said that "the spirits of the prophets are subject to the control of prophets" (I Corinthians 14:32). This means you can't just spout off what and when you want, and when challenged, wash your hands of responsibility by saying, "Well, when the Spirit comes upon me, I can't help what comes out!"

This approach seems to assume that when God's Spirit moves us, we're fully mature, seasoned, and flawless vessels. This is arrogant, and is in itself a sign that we have a lot of growing up to do.

So let's do it. Let's start growing up into this today!

*

TRY THIS!

The best way to receive training on the prophetic is to study the Bible, learning from the prophetic experience of people who travelled this journey before you. In particular, study Matthew, Mark, Luke, and John, learning from the Ultimate Prophet, Jesus Christ. Once you realize he is a Prophet, you'll see him being prophetic on pretty much every page, and he does it all—words of knowledge, words of wisdom, prophecy about the future... it's awesome!

A secondary way to receive training in the prophetic is to spend time with someone who has developed their prophetic ministry or gift and learn from them. If you don't know someone like that, you can try reading a good book about it, like these two:

Translating God, by Shawn Bolz

Basic Training for the Prophetic Ministry, by Kris Vallotton

Both of these guys are gifted in ways I can't even begin to describe or claim for myself.

SPECIALTIES & GIFTING

As you practice sharing your prophetic messages with people over time and track how they are received, you'll probably notice interesting patterns emerging.

Some prophetic people get pictures from God more than any kind of other message. Others may receive single words, others may get sentences, others may get Bible verses to share that hit the bulls-eye, and still others may get all kinds of pictures or analogies that mirror people's lives. God speaks in all kinds of ways!

In other words, over time you'll develop a kind of specialty. This doesn't mean you can never step out of your specialty. Think of it as God's favourite way to use you in the prophetic. Also know that specialties can change over time as God brings new things to life in you.

Prophetic specialties sometimes include specific subjects or topics. I've heard stories of prophets who's messages about finances or business tend to be off base, but when they speak into relationships they tend to be bang on, for example.

If you're tracking your messages and receiving correction along the way, you may notice a topical pattern like this emerge in your own life. Don't try to read too much into it, but if the pattern seems to be there, talk to God about it. It could be he's trying to focus your ministry on something more specific.

A third way you may notice a speciality emerging is in the type of prophetic message you bring: words of knowledge, words of wisdom, or prophecies about the future. If you need to refresh your memory about what those are, you can find the definitions starting on page 36.

I've noticed a clear pattern or specialty in my own life. I don't get very many words of knowledge or words about the future, but I get a lot of words of wisdom to share. That's my specialty. This doesn't mean I can never venture outside that speciality. My specialty isn't a box to confine me; it's a sweet spot to focus me.

Since God urges us to pursue prophecy and to be eager to prophesy, it's probably a good idea to ask God to increase your effectiveness and develop elements in you that you still lack. I've been asking God to give me more words of knowledge lately, especially as I share my faith with people who don't believe in Jesus. It hasn't happened yet, but I'm still asking!

A fourth way a specialty emerges relates to the area of spiritual gifts. While everyone is called to be prophetic, some members of Christ's family are supernaturally gifted in the prophetic:

> "Now to each one the manifestation of the Spirit is given for the common good. To one there is given through the Spirit a message of wisdom, to another a message of knowledge by means of the same Spirit... to another prophecy... All these are the work of one and the same Spirit, and he distributes them to each one, just as he determines" (I Corinthians 12: 7-11).

Prophetic people generally give messages to other people. A person with the gift of prophecy also gives messages to people, but they also give messages to *groups* of people. The most comprehensive instructions about using the gift of prophecy are found in I Corinthians 14. Here is a snippet from that chapter:

> "Two or three prophets should speak, and the others should weigh carefully what is said. And if a revelation comes to someone who is sitting down, the first speaker should stop. For you can all prophesy in turn so that everyone may be instructed and encouraged. The spirits of prophets are subject to the control of prophets. For God is not a God of disorder but of peace—as in all the congregations of the Lord's people" (I Corinthians 14:29-33)

How do you know if you have the gift of prophecy? Samuel, a little boy in the Old Testament, received a gift and calling as a prophet. Here's how it played out for him:

"The Lord was with Samuel as he grew up, and he let none of Samuel's words fall to the ground. And all Israel from Dan to Beersheba recognized that Samuel was attested as a prophet of the Lord" (I Samuel 3:19,20).

We can see two markers of true prophets by studying this season of Samuel's life: First, he experienced a degree of accuracy in his prophetic messages that pointed to a special calling. Second, the people around him recognized that giftedness and calling and affirmed it. The same thing happens today.

Don't worry too much about whether you're gifted in prophecy. Just love people; ask God to develop prophetic power in your life so you can speak words that strengthen, encourage, and comfort. Let people correct you and train you. And then, over time, ask God to help you connect the dots to identify specialties and gifting.

I haven't spent much time on the gift of prophecy in this book. That's because I wrote it for average Joes like me who probably don't have the gift but are called to be prophetic as a way of life. I hope this book has inspired you, clarified what being prophetic means, and motivated you to step out in faith as God awakens this calling in you.

*

TRY THIS!

Well, it's time for you to stretch your wings and jump out of the nest! Let me remind you of the fulfillment of Joel's ancient prophecy:

"This is what was spoken by the prophet Joel: 'In the last days, God says, "I will pour out my Spirit on all people. Your sons and daughters will prophesy, your young men will see visions, your old men will dream dreams. Even on my servants, both men and women, I will pour out my Spirit in those days, and they will prophesy" (Acts 2:16-18).

These are "those days." You are those people. You are among those servants.

It's your turn to become a fulfillment of Joel's prophecy.
Go.

Be.

Prophetic.

I'm cheering for you!

Other Books By Brad Huebert on Amazon

Now What? Making the Most of Your First Forty Days in Christ is a powerful introduction to faith in Jesus for people who just gave their lives to him, grounding new believers in forty days of biblical truth. It's also life-changing for people who's faith has gotten stale and need a personal renewal.

Beloved: Some Fairy Tales Are True is a recasting of the epic biblical story in the form of a fairy tale. Discover the heart of the Christian faith from a new angle—or recapture your love for Jesus in this fresh look at the ancient story. Some fairy tales… are true!

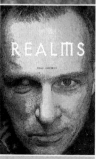

Realms is a fantasy allegory written to set you free from lifeless religion. What if you woke up one day to find yourself in the spiritual realm, where all the things you took by faith were suddenly visible to your eyes? What would have to change? Where would that journey take you? One thing is certain: You would never be the same.

Go With The Flow: A Non-Religious Approach To Your Daily Time With God unpacks a simple and yet powerful approach to spending time with God that will infuse your life with new life and purpose. Discover a natural pathway designed by God to set you free to enjoy him!

Made in the USA
Charleston, SC
29 November 2016